ROLF HARRIS PERSONALITY CATS

Rolf Harris
Personality Cats

TEXT BY
Rolf and Alwen Harris

PHOTOGRAPHY AND CARTOONS BY
Rolf Harris

Anaya Publishers

First Published in Great Britain by Anaya Publishers Ltd,
Strode House, 44–50 Osnaburgh Street, London NW1 3ND

Editor: Katherine Yeates
Design: Hammond Hammond

British Library Cataloguing in Publication Data

Harris, Rolf
Rolf Harris personality cats.
I. Title
636.8

ISBN 1–85470–133–9

Phototypeset in Century Old Style by Intype, London
Colour reproduction by Scantrans Pte. Ltd., Singapore
Printed and bound in Hong Kong

INTRODUCTION

Many wife Alwen and I have written this book as a joint effort. It's been a wonderful exercise and has had the effect of bringing us even closer together. You'd be amazed at the vast number of memories we've conjured up.

What about us? We've been married for over thirty years. In all those years we've had cats sharing our lives, sometimes as many as *fourteen* at once, so you can imagine how much joy and laughter and sadness go hand in hand as we think back.

There is a convention I've used in writing this book. When there is a direct quotation from Al, it's in single inverted commas, like this, 'Oh, don't forget to mention that Foxy Lady used to come down the road with me, sitting on my shoulders, whenever I posted letters.' When there are no direct quotes, it's me talking to you. Hope that makes sense.

Our two lives have been so vastly different. Alwen grew up in the UK and was only a youngster when the Second World War started. I was just a bit older, on the other side of the world in Western Australia, with no experience of that war other than what I read in newspapers or heard on the radio.

We only seem to have had one thing in common in those childhood years. We were both surrounded by cats and dogs as household pets, and

Alwen holding our new young 'Ginger Jobs', Toffee, the adventurous one on the left and Toad, the baby.

•

All cats love the security of a cardboard box around them.

7

both grew up completely at ease in their company. It's a good feeling.

My first cat was simply called Pussy. I can never remember a time when she wasn't there during my childhood. When I left to come to England in 1952, Pussy was twenty years old, with no teeth and white eyebrows on her tabby fur, but still producing kittens. A lot of other cats passed through my life, but old Puss was a constant through that time. Dad was more at ease with dogs than with cats, and would not allow cats in the house, whereas Mum was very fond of them all. Over to you, Alwen.

'Well, I was the same, always had cats and dogs around me as a child. The first cat I can remember, was a black fluffy thing called Smut, Smuts or Smutty. The main memory I have of her was when I shut the door and took off a small piece of the end of her tail. I was only a tiny child when it happened, but I can still remember my feelings of horror and remorse. It was awful! I shudder to think of it still.

'It was mainly my dog that I played with. I suppose ordinary cats were aloof and independent by comparison. Dogs really loved you for yourself and wanted to be with you all the time.

'My first dog was a big Airedale called Squibs and we were inseparable. We always slept together. If ever you couldn't find me, you just had to look in the dog basket or inside the kennel. Nine times out of ten, I would be there, curled up with Squibs, fast asleep. I shared her bones and used to run on all fours with her, even up and down stairs. I was about six or seven years of age by then. She protected me. When I was a baby, this big Airedale wouldn't let anyone *near* my pram. Nobody was allowed to even look in it! It was wonderful. I was absolutely devastated when she died. As a child, you think animals are going to be there for ever.

'Sorry, this book is supposed to be about cats isn't it. My grandfather bought me this long-haired blue Persian cat for five pounds. We called her Shah. He bought her under rather suspicious circumstances, I think. Man in the street with this lovely cat under his coat . . .'

Fell off the back of a lorry?

'Yes, possibly! She was absolutely superb. She grew to be enormous. We took her to Wales when the war started, and we left her with an aunt. My mother felt she really couldn't look after a cat in London, with it always needing attention. There was my tiny baby brother and me so she was duly left. My aunt used to write and let us know about Shah and how she was getting on.

'When we moved away from London to the farm up in the Lake District, they didn't have cats as pets. Cats were working animals living in the barns keeping the mouse population at bay. They were quite wild, so all my affection for animals turned to the ponies and the cows. I was always happier with them than with people. You could be really quiet and they would come up and sniff you, accept you, and from then on, treat you as one of them. There is nothing more calming than to be with a herd of cows when they're sitting chewing the cud. I'm off the subject of cats again. Back to you.'

Well, when I think back, it never occurred to me as a child, that different cats might have different personalities. I only felt that some were smarter than others, some really stupid.

CATS AND CAMERAS

'Talk about the photographs you've taken for the book.'

Right. Well, I've always drawn for as long as I can remember, but photography as a serious hobby only came after we got married.

I'd borrowed cameras before that time, sometimes quite expensive ones, but I'd never understood them. As a result, I usually produced below average, out of focus, 'snaps', and that's all you could call them.

Ratbag loved to soak up the sun, and quite often got sunburnt as a result.

Foxy Lady basks in the
sunlight, while
checking the goings-on
in the outside world.

•

Purr Shah Pudding
reckons this beats
television any day.

When Alwen and I were heading out to Australia in 1959, our ship stopped at Aden and I thought, 'I should really get a decent camera duty free and learn how to use it.' Decent! Wow! The bloke talked me into buying the best. I got a Rolleiflex *and* an attachment for taking 35mm film for only forty-one pounds! It seemed an awful lot of money to me at the time, but looking back, wasn't that money well spent! I studied the book of words and over the next year, really got to know all about focus, shutter speed, film speed, lens aperture and depth of field, and how they all inter-related. It was a revelation.

When photographing cats, there's a trick Alwen and I use. It should interest you if you have a passion for cats and cameras.

Get yourself and your camera all organized. Work out your shutter speed, and if possible get the focusing all done in advance, so that the cat is pin sharp in your viewfinder, and then – and this is the trick – you do one of two things. You either pant realistically like a dog, or you miaow like some other 'stranger' cat. If your ability as a mimic is any good, your cat's head will shoot up, eyes wide and alert. There it will stay, absolutely motionless looking directly at you, trying to see where on earth this dog or cat is.

NOW WHERE'S THAT BLASTED CAT?

INTRODUCTION

During that split second when all movement is frozen, if you haven't taken the shot you ought to be kicked.

This trick is especially valuable in low light conditions. You can grab a shot at, say, one fifteenth of a second (if you can hold the camera steady enough), and the cat won't have moved at all in that time. Mind you, cats aren't stupid. You can't catch them too many times with the same ruse. But I promise you it does work wonders.

If you want the cat looking somewhere other than directly at the camera, get your partner to pant or bark or miaow from a different position. (Of course it helps if you are as mad as we are!) If you feel stupid doing it all, *just wait 'til you see the slides back*!

'We have quite a few photographers around to take shots and they always want the cats in the picture with us. The photographers try to arrange poses, which just doesn't work with animals. If you're going to do it right, you've got to get in the position, get everything organized to the cameraman's satisfaction, and remember that pose. *Then* get the cats, and the photographer must just take shots!

'On one occasion a photographer was arranging and rearranging the cats as if they were objects that would stay put, and I'm afraid I lost my cool. I told him, "For goodness sake get behind your camera and get on with the job!" In no uncertain terms . . . (chuckle) . . .

'Cats get bored. And they get ratty. They really get up tight, and I don't blame them because I'm the same. I get up tight. They don't like the flash going off. It's all strange to them. All they want to do is explore and find out about everything.'

13

*Purr Shah Pudding
spring cleaning.*

They just get fed up and want to be somewhere else.

'Yes, they've had enough. They've got other things they want to do.'

I must say I really dislike using flash, much prefer available light. Train yourself to stand feet astride, arms with elbows locked in to your ribs, camera clenched rock steady in your left hand. Next, take a breath and hold it, and then, when your finger slowly but firmly pushes down the release button, you'd be amazed at the slow shutter speeds you can successfully use.

A lot of people stab at the button and wonder why their shots always seem a bit blurry. You don't have to rush that action. The mechanism inside your camera does all the speed bit.

When you stab at it, the jolt rotates the camera slightly in your left hand, and this is happening just when the shutter is open. If you have one of these shots enlarged, you'll find that the focus isn't the reason for it looking blurred. Your focus may be perfect, but everything has moved in a slight curve while your shutter has been open and *that* is what has registered on the film.

It's no good using the old 'I'm no good with cameras' excuse. Go away and get the 'book of words', find out how *your* camera works, and *get* to be good!

DRAWING CATS

Drawing cats is another matter. I can't tell you how to draw. A lot of it is confidence brought about by encouragement from parents and teachers, and a lot of it is observation. A lot of it is inherited talent too, I'm sure. If you are fairly good at drawing in a realistic way, then a good way to practise is to draw the cat while never taking your eye off the animal. Cats move to a new position so frequently (unless they're sleeping). You've got to capture what you can while you can.

You're probably saying, 'What d'you mean never take your eye

Various sketches of a sleepy Toffee.

off? How can I draw if I don't keep looking back to the paper all the time?'

All I can tell you is that it works. It frees your 'line' incredibly. You start to forget about making a pretty, finished picture. You start to *look*, and to *see*, and to note down *what* you see, quickly and efficiently, before the mog has moved.

You can do your finished drawings later from your notes if you wish, but I think you'll start to like the spontaneity of the first sketch better. Alwen?

'I've never drawn cats. I've always drawn horses and cows. I go and observe them. They're forever on the move, so you can't sit to draw, and anyway, paper always frightens them. I used to draw wild horses on Dartmoor and the whiteness of a sheet of paper and the wind flapping it about spooks them. If you can keep it very still they'll come and see what it is. They come right up to you and they sniff you all over, and the paper too. They examine it. It's super. No, usually I would just sit with them and watch them carry on. Draw them from memory when I got back.'

Do you find cats much the same, very curious?

'Well, the Devon Rexes, yes. Compared to moggies, I think thoroughbred cats are much more interesting *and* interested. Mogs are very . . .'

Getting on with the business of living?

'Yes. They're independent, whereas all the Devons I've known, they rely on you totally, for everything. They're just like the dogs I had as a child. They like to be with you, all the time, and they *hate* it when you go away. They don't "speak" to you when you come back sometimes. Rats used to turn his back and purposely ignore you, rather like my dog Puggy did. Throw out an "atmosphere". And they look at you very suspiciously for quite a while.

'They also like to meet you at the door. The two little Ginger

Toffee, the adventurer, checks on a bumble bee while Toad keeps his distance and watches.

INTRODUCTION

Jobs we've got now, Toffee and Toad, they hear the car coming and they run to meet you. They're there behind the door, waiting. They watch out of the window to see where we're going and what we're up to, and they watch for us to come back. It's lovely.'

Back to drawing cats. Today, you can take video of fast moving action and then 'freeze' that picture on the play-back screen. It's still a good idea, though, to use the 'eye permanently on the model' trick when drawing from the screen, even though you do have the pose held motionless.

A cartoon drawing of a cat, well that's another thing entirely. You should always base the cartoon on the reality of the animal in front of you, but try to get the comedy by maybe relating the cat's actions to what a human's actions might be in the same circumstances. You may even put in human expressions, like smiling, or frowning, to show what the cat is feeling in a way people will recognize.

Observation is the answer. Try to see what the cats do to signal their changing moods. How do they look when they're angry or when they're contented? What are the differences that characterise different cats, and different breeds? See if you can caricature those differences, and look at the work of other cartoonists. There may be some ideas there that you can use.

'Enough! Rolf and I hope you enjoy our book of PERSONALITY CATS.'

Samantha Mouse

Miss Samantha Mouse, eventually just known as Mouse, was our very first Devon Rex. She joined the household in 1975. In Alwen's words, 'I saw her first in a cat show. This face was peeping out of a white blanket, and I'd never seen a Devon Rex before. I could not tear my eyes away from her.'

'Clear as crystal in my mind, up popped an image from a book about animals that I'd loved as a tiny girl. There was one picture in it of a Fenec Fox, and it had such huge ears and such big round saucer-shaped eyes, just to look at it would send me into gales of laughter. My mother would laugh at my laughter, and soon we would both be hysterical, and all because of the picture of this startled-looking animal.'

'Now here was a little cat peering up at me with big eyes and huge ears, taking

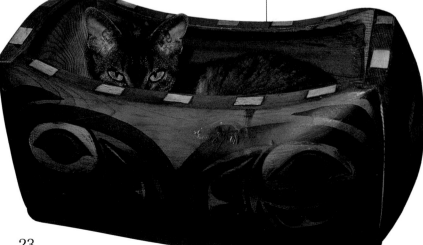

The young and old Mouse. We particularly loved the two sets of eyes in the Canadian Indian box.

me back to that photograph.

'I couldn't wait to find the owner and ask if she was for sale. She was, and I had to have her there and then. I couldn't wait to show everyone when I brought her home. I loved her. I remember saying to my Mum and Dad, "Look what I've got," and they said, "Whatever is it?" They couldn't believe it.

'She looked lovely. We could take her anywhere in the car and she adored it. In her collar and lead she would sit there, loving it.'

Later, when our next two Rex kittens arrived, her nose was put right out of joint. She just would not accept them. We gave her to Alwen's Mum and Dad who looked after her and loved her. She's back in the house now, as a geriatric old lady and she's fine. She's holding her own. Bosses everybody about.

When Alwen's father was in a home, we used to take her over to see him and that was the only time she would have milk. She would be waiting on tenterhooks for the tea trolley to be brought in, because the nurse, by prior arrangement, would have a saucer especially for her. She would really hoe into that milk.

'We used to make fun of her going to tea with Grandpa. She'll rarely take any notice of milk, but there she would have a saucer-full. She was really waiting too. If anybody came in, she would be up, pestering them for her treat.

'She loves guests. She was mightily put out the other day because somebody arrived to see Rolf and the two of them went straight into the office. Dear seventeen-year-old Mouse moved her old bones from her warm spot by the stove in the kitchen. Off she

24

struggled to the office door to see who'd arrived, and to find out why they hadn't come to see her.'

She gets up from her sleeping place whenever you're sitting down and comes creaking over for a visit. A little plaintive 'miaow' at your elbow alerts you and you have to help her up on to your lap for a cuddle. If you caress her under the chin she thrusts her head forward, sort of clenches her nostrils shut, closes her eyes, and goes off into seventh heaven, purring motor running full bore.

'When guests come, she *has* to climb up on to their laps, but must be a bit of a shock to them, because she looks so scruffy. She is the image of "Mogwai", the character out of the film *Gremlins*.'

She rules the roost, even though she *is* seventeen. Any other cat that gets in her way, or tries to pinch her sleeping spot, the 'swearing' starts. Talk about a growl! Everybody gives her a wide berth when that tetchy disgruntled row starts up. It's sad to see how old and infirm she's getting, though. Sometimes she shakes her head from side to side, like a dog shedding water after a swim, and the force of the shake almost throws her off her feet. The stumbling steps to the side and the shaky recovery of balance are very amusing to watch, but very sad at the same time, and you dread the day when she goes. What a gap she'll leave. When she's not by the stove, she's on her heated pad. (Rexes feel the cold.) She always sleeps on her right side, and all the fur has gone on that side. Poor old Mouse. She looks really lop-sided. What a picture when Alwen gives her a bath.

Mouse as a kitten with a tiny bell on her collar and as she is today, a very old lady.

Mouse watches a bee struggling in the swimming pool.

A Special Breed of Cat

Once we had Samantha Mouse, we were really smitten with the Devon Rex breed. They are a totally different sort of cat to any other cat we've ever had. They thrive on the company of humans. I've said it before, but they love to be with you always, and the closer the better. Their favourite position is sitting on your shoulder, leaning and snuggling against your neck, or better still, sitting in your lap, with their head under your chin. If you don't relish this sort of close contact, the sort of devotion and companionship you expect from a very loving dog . . . then don't get a Devon Rex.

There is a special feature about Devon Rexes that might interest people who are allergic to cats. Devon Rex fur is totally different to the fur on any other cat. For some reason the thing that causes all those allergic reactions is missing. People just don't get the blocked sinuses and the red and weeping eyes when they're around Devon Rexes.

We've persuaded quite a few people to become Devon Rex owners. One friend in particular used to have to insist on our non-Rex cats being shut in another room when he and his wife came to

Toffee and Toad up a tree and Toad snuggling up with his sister Charcoal.

*Toad in the garden,
and curled up with his
sisters Little Owl and
Charcoal.*

visit us, otherwise the day was a misery for him. They now share their lives with two marvellous Rexes, Monty and Caspar, and couldn't be happier.

You should *see* a Devon Rex when it's happy. It's the opposite of any other cat you've ever seen. If you're a cat person, and know a bit about the signals cats give out, you'll know that as soon as they start to thrash their tails about, they are getting really angry and if you don't stop what you're doing to annoy them, they'll eventually 'spag' you with their claws and get the heck out of it.

With a Devon Rex, when they wag their tail, they're really happy and when they are *really*, *really* happy, they wag their whole body. As we write this, up pops a clear as crystal mental picture of Ratbag the day he'd won best of breed and was being considered for best of show. He was strolling up and down the table pleased as punch, just 'waggling' from front to back. People were laughing with pleasure at his pleasure, if you know what I mean.

The only reason he wasn't given best of breed, the judge told us afterwards, was because he had no fur at all. (See Trade Descriptions Act!)

'We keep talking about Devon Rex cats, rather than Rex cats. It's because we don't know anything about the Cornish Rex. Never had any contact with them.'

Fluffy Britches and Weed shut out in the greenhouse with the Rexes, Ratbag, Foxy and Kipper, waiting anxiously for their dinner.

The Devon Rex, as a breed, appeared as recently as 1960 (Cornish Rexes – about 1950). As I understand it, a lady named Beryl Cox became aware of a strangely different kitten in amongst a bunch of wild kittens. She was captivated by this one special curly-coated kitten. It was blue, long-legged, with a pixie-shaped face, and was totally different in personality to the others.

Where the other kittens would take off like the wild creatures they were every time she got too close, this special one showed great curiosity, and eventually Beryl was able to coax it away from

32

the rest. She called it 'Kirlee' and they adopted each other. It moved in with her and became a loving member of the household.

By chance, Beryl happened to read about a new breed of cat called Cornish Rex. One of the features of the breed was that it had a curly coat, and Beryl assumed that her Kirlee was the same type of cat. She contacted Mr Stirling-Webb, the noted breeder and geneticist, who suggested that Kirlee be mated with one of the offspring of Kallibunker, the first Cornish Rex.

Well, to his disappointment, the resulting kittens were straight-coated. Kirlee was a different Rex mutation altogether, to be designated Devon Rex.

Subsequent breeding experiments were carried out with both the Cornish and the Devon Rex by the lovely Alison Ashford (a close friend of ours), and she proved beyond doubt that each genotype was unique.

'There's one thing Devon Rexes do that we've got used to now – well, I have. Rolf's never ready for it when it happens. Let me explain. You're standing with your back to them, reasonably close – say, four to five feet away – and they can't see what you're doing. They will take off from wherever they are and land on your shoulders, or half way up your back.

'You can understand their thinking. What you're secretively doing might just involve FOOD! As I said, we've got used to it, but guests get the shock of their lives to have this sudden weight land on them unannounced. (Usually with claws out to avoid the possibility of falling!)'

Their passion for food and intense curiosity are two Rex characteristics which have led to many a funny story. We have included a few of the best but there are so many others which still make us laugh.

*Toffee as a baby
and compact,
sleeping Ratbag.*

Ratbag and Smudge

Ratbag, below, and drawings of Ratbag and his sister Smudge.

W e can't remember how we first heard about this special 'bald' Devon Rex. Probably at one of the cat shows. I know that Alwen was fascinated by the stories she'd heard and wanted to see for herself.

I couldn't go, I was working, but Alwen got a friend of hers to drive her up to Nottingham and they met Barbara Hudson, the breeder. They were ushered into the front room and there was a heap of Devon Rex kittens playing on the floor. Barbara made coffee, and they sat down by the fire, and just watched the kittens.

'We were sitting chatting, and this kitten, this fascinating naked creature with huge ears, got up, walked over to me, walked straight up the front of me and went behind my hair. Then another one with a normal Rex coat came up and did the same thing. The others took no notice of me at all. It was just these two, brother and sister, sitting on my shoulders, hiding behind my hair, which I wore quite long at the time.

'I kept getting them down from there and putting them on my lap because I wanted to see them close to, but at every opportunity they were back on my shoulders. It was

36

Ratbag drinking out of a full cup, sending water splashing everywhere, and curled up and hiding, half asleep.

enchanting. We enjoyed their antics for about ten minutes, and then put them down while we went out to the cattery to see some more cats and kittens.

'When we came back in, I leant over the back of the couch to look at all the kittens and these same two came up over the front, straight on to my shoulders and settled down again. Without consciously planning it, I suddenly turned to Barbara and said, "Well, that's it. I'll just have to buy the two!"

'They were sent down later by train because they weren't old enough at the time to leave their mother. I remember we got a taxi to King's Cross station to collect these two tiny things. I knew how Samantha Mouse loved warmth, and here was this little male arriving with virtually no hair on him at all! I had a basket for them with two blankets *and* a hot water bottle, and just hoped that that would be enough.

Ratbag pretending to be ET.

'That very special naked little boy we called Ratbag, because, as Rolf said, "What else could you call him?" His sister was Smudge. There were fancy pedigree names of course, but we never used them.'

There was always a very special bond between Alwen and Ratbag (or Rats, as we called him). This sort of togetherness, this fusion of spirits, had happened once before with Alwen. She had owned a slim, black, standard poodle when we first met. Pugs was her name, and when we got married, Puggy, wearing a brand new red leather collar and lead for the occasion, went very proudly up the aisle with Alwen as her only bridesmaid.

Pugsy, and later, Rats, were Alwen's soul mates. There are no other words for the bond that existed between them. Dear old Ratty was something special. There are times even now, years afterwards, when I will suddenly find Alwen in tears. 'What's wrong?' I ask, and she says, 'I just miss Rats so *much*!'

RATBAG AND SMUDGE

It's hard to describe the enormous sense of loss we still both feel when we think of that marvellous personality cat. Never been a cat like him! His skin was like velvet and to hold him was like holding a hot peach.

The day he got best of breed in the cat show, he definitely knew what was going on. He was up there on the table in front of all those people 'strutting his stuff' like you've never seen! His whole body was smiling, it was pretty to watch.

'We took Ratbag to a television studio once for an interview about Devon Rexes. We had a see-through plastic cat basket, and everybody was looking at him. "What on earth is that?" Poor Rats. We were continuously explaining it was a cat. "What sort of cat is it?"

'I even took him to a vet once who thought he was a Chihuahua!'

People used to say, 'What *have* you done to that poor cat? Fancy shaving off all its fur!'

' . . . Or "Has he got a skin disease?" I still have comments now, even with well-coated Rexes, like "How could you curl that poor cat's hair?" Rats, with no hair at all, used to get sunburned and his skin actually peeled on one occasion.'

Back to the interview story.

'Oh yes, I took him around the studio on a collar and lead. He examined everything and looked at everybody, and when it was his turn to come and sit down, he'd seen the lot and was quite happy . . . until the "giraffe" thing arrived . . . '

That's the boom microphone. It's a contraption on wheels with a platform the operator stands on, and this great long neck snakes out above you with a movable 'mike' on the end. This can be swivelled from side to side to favour whoever's talking at the time.

Check those wrinkles!

41

Was that a squirrel?
YES, IT IS A
SQUIRREL!

'He hadn't seen that before, and he had to stand on his hind legs to reach up to try and get it. As the microphone moved from side to side it was enchanting to see his reaction, stood full stretch with his "arms" out.'

I called up to the people in the control room, 'Get a shot of the cat!' They only had us and the interviewer on screen and there was this mesmerising, once-in-a-lifetime bit of action going to waste. 'Cut to the cat!' I shouted to them again, so they finally did and they had shots of this magic cat, on its hind legs.

'. . . Head looking up, trying to reach far enough to get hold of the microphone. It was beautiful. We asked them for a video-tape, which they were nice enough to send, but when we played it back, it was the wrong one! What a pity not to have a tape of that sequence with Rats. Lovely to watch that Rex curiosity.'

Rats and Smudge were notorious food-swipers. On one memorable occasion, Alwen cooked a huge spaghetti marrow and we'd eaten half of it. We left the other half on the kitchen table (which one never does when one has Devon Rex cats). We ate the meal and Alwen came out into the kitchen to find this mess on the floor.

Rats had 'spagged' this half marrow, pulled it down and was busy eating it. We watched in utter amazement as he sucked up the strands one at a time, just as if it *was* spaghetti. He was thoroughly enjoying himself.

'Rolf had brought back a take-away curry for a house load of guests, and a bag full of poppadoms was placed on the table. Quick as a flash, Smudge had hooked the bag off the table and the lot spilled out and shot all over the place. Rexes have no guilty feelings concerning food. They just know that they're probably going to be shouted at and stopped at any moment, so they eat like lightning.

'In this instance, Smudge

44

proceeded to pounce on them and eat them as fast as she could. There were tiny bits of poppadom all over the place. The floor looked as if snow had been falling, and the crunching noise as she frantically bit into each new piece would have been something marvellous to listen to if we could have heard it over the laughter.'

On another occasion we had some guests in for drinks and Alwen had put some crisps out on a dish on a small table. Smudge, from her vantage point under the table, snakes a little paw up and hooks the edge of the plate. Well, down the plate came, hit the carpet on its edge and the crisps shot from here to Kingdom Come!

All the Devons will stand inside a window and 'chatter' at birds that are outside. They catch sight of a bird, their tail thrashes around, and they make this enchanting high pitched sort of 'yayayaya' sound. Their bottom jaw is jerking up and down as they 'say' it. You wonder what's going through their minds. What are they saying? 'If only I could get out through this glass, I'd give you what for!'

Smudge used to do that same sound during her special game.
She would play what we called 'Peek-a-boo' with us. Lying in bed in the morning was an ideal time. Smudgey would be waiting for you to rise (and get the cat food, of course). You only had to make a very obvious move to put yourself down out of her direct line of vision, and the game was on!

You'd wait a second, then reappear in a slightly different spot. Her eyes would whip across to where you were, and her jaw would open and close rapidly as she did that 'yayayaya' chattering. Keeping eye contact with her, drop down out of sight, and then pop up again in some unexpected spot and she was always there, her wide eyes fixed right on you and 'yayayaya', she'd go again. She loved the game, and would play it for as long as you could be bothered. I never ever saw her get fed up with this 'human's foolishness'.

Foxy Lady

We mated Smudge with a ginger Devon Rex male and she had two black kittens and two tortoiseshell ones. They were born the day Mrs Thatcher became Prime Minister. I remember because we were listening to the reporting of the events on the radio, and Smudgey was very, very restless and Rats kept licking her. Lick, lick, lick, it was very moving to see his concern. Poor old Rats. He got himself in such a state with trying to help her, we finally had to put him downstairs and shut the door.

Smudge wouldn't let Alwen get up. They were on the bed, and people had to keep giving Alwen cups of tea and eventually Smudge had her kittens under Alwen's dressing gown. To get up and go to the toilet, Alwen had to struggle out of her dressing gown and keep it over Smudge so that she would still have that reassuring warmth and recognisable scent all around her.

The kittens finally arrived, there, under the dressing gown on the bed. But some little while later, when it appeared to be all over, our daughter Bindi said, 'She feels as if she's got another one in there.' 'No, no,' said Alwen quite confidently.

It was the next day, at least eighteen hours later, that Alwen got the surprise. She looked at Smudge, and there was a little orange-coloured foot just becoming visible.

'It was a back foot and I knew it was a breach birth, so I helped this little thing out. Soggy Biscuit I called it, for obvious reasons. That's just what it looked like. Anyway, nothing was happening, no

Is this a good pose?

47

movement, nothing at all.'

The kitten appeared to be lifeless, so Alwen filled the bathroom sink, lowered the still little thing into the warm water and gave it mouth to mouth resuscitation. Amazingly, it came round.

'I dried it, held it over the radiator in my hand and phoned the vet. He wasn't much help, just told me to keep doing what I was doing, so I kept the little mite warm and then rubbed it all over Smudgey. I pretended I was stroking her, because I realised that Soggy's special kitten smell must have all gone with the warm water and the drying, and Smudge wouldn't know it was hers. I thought "Oh dear", so I rubbed the kitten all over her back, where she couldn't see what I was up to.

'Then we couldn't get it to suckle. I got a small eye dropper, made up a mixture and kept feeding the little thing, and later the next day we managed to get her on to Smudge's teat. She thrived, and grew up to be the brightest of the lot of them! We renamed her Foxy Lady. What a fitting name! If anything was happening, anything at all, it *had* to be Foxy Lady!

'Rats used to look after Smudge's kittens, used to "kitten-sit". He didn't mind them trying to suckle him. In fact, he used to like it immensely. I've never seen a male cat be so affectionate towards kittens. It was marvellous.

Kipper at ease.

'We kept Foxy Lady and sold the others. One was called Gentle. Oh yes, we also kept the black one, called Mr Mole. Unfortunately, as time went on, he got very aggressive. He wanted you to focus only on him. He was never happier than when he was the centre of attention and we were ignoring the others. As soon as you spent time with any one of the other cats, he would start "swearing" and would attack them all! He was generally becoming a real grouch.'

After much soul searching, we gave him to friends of ours, and they really loved him. They had another cat, a long-haired Persian. As she wasn't a Rex, and so, I guess, posed no threat to Mole, he was as happy as Larry from then on, a different cat.

Foxy Lady later had kittens of her own and we kept one of her daughters, Kipper. The Ginger Jobs we called Foxy and Kipper. What a pair of terrors! Fox opened doors by jumping up and hanging on to the horizontal handle, which would then turn as she slid down it. At the same time she would kick off the wall with her hind legs.

I tried time after time to capture this on movie, but of course, when I had it all ready, she wouldn't even consider opening the door. The moment the camera's put away, she's up on to the handle again, naturally!

A boat full of visitors moors in front of the house. Before you can say 'MacPhirtlesquirt's squashed squid', the Ginger Jobs are on the boat like a streak of light and off again, each with a sandwich in her mouth from the buffet laid out on board.

Foxy comes galumphing out of someone's house on a Sunday with an uncooked leg of lamb in her mouth. She looks for all the world like a lioness dragging her prey in some wildlife film. But now what do we do? We didn't see which house she came from. Oh dear!

None of the other Rexes seemed to want to explore beyond the confines of our safe bit of home territory, but Foxy Lady used to range far and wide. One day she came racing down the road from one of these expeditions with a food pack, all plastic wrapped, containing tandoori chicken.

I tried to catch her once again, but as usual, she easily evaded me, dived under a bush where I couldn't go, and ran, leaving the package there. I scraped my way in amongst the spiky branches and retrieved it, only to find to my stunned amazement that she'd somehow broken the plastic and taken the contents in the short time she'd been out of my sight.

Where she got the food parcel from was a mystery. There was

There's a lovely sense of safety in the sink for Kipper. It's like being in a cardboard box.

•

She loved smelling blossoms.

no hue and cry and no vengeful pursuit of any sort. Perhaps she was in a window and out again with her booty before anyone noticed. You can imagine some poor bemused lady in a kitchen somewhere, scratching her head and saying, 'I'm sure I got a pack of curried chook. Where on earth did I put it?' What amazes me is, how did Fox know it was edible, all plastic wrapped and sealed in there?

'She probably read the label I guess!' says Alwen.

All this reminds me of an occasion that happened when we were away. We were due home from holiday and the friends, who were looking after our house and our multitude of cats, decided to welcome us back with a lovely meal. It was going to be more like a banquet really, because the people we had been staying with in France were coming back with us in the car. There was going to be quite a large group to feed.

When we got back, we couldn't believe the story, well, until we saw the cats, that is. Here's what had happened. During the day, David and Elizabeth had prepared a huge meal with a fifteen-pound turkey, sausages and lots of other goodies. They were stuck for a place to cool the food where our permanently ravenous cats couldn't get at it. Eventually they thought of spreading it out down in the laundry area. There was a closable door there. Good thinking.

The cats followed their every move as they got all the food moved to this 'safe' place. They had to be continually shooed away and brushed off. Elizabeth said later that she was always very conscious of Foxy Lady watching everything she did with eagle eyes. It unnerved her at the time.

They had to go out to the shops for something, and when they got back, Elizabeth thought, 'Surely I closed that door.' She went down into the laundry room and wondered what on earth Foxy Lady and Kipper were doing lying on their backs with their legs pointing upwards and outwards. They looked for all the world like bloated Bhuddas.

Horror of
horrors, they had
eaten everything.
Everything! All
that preparation and it was inside
the two Ginger Terrors. Mother
and daughter had really done a
demolition job on the banquet.

They struggled up into a sitting position and
tried to move, and Elizabeth actually had to help
them to roll forward onto their feet so they could
walk. She was furious, but at the same time, she
couldn't help laughing. The cats made such a comical picture trying
to drag their stomachs up the steps. The skin was all stretched and
shiny with each individual hair seeming to occupy about a square
centimetre of otherwise bare space. Their bulging bellies actually
dragged along the floor as they moved.

I suppose we should have warned Lizzie that Fox could turn that
sort of handle and open doors, but it never occurred to us to do so.

(Oh yes. Most of our Devons climb and swing around on curtains
and do a bit of shredding, so be warned all you potential Devon Rex
owners. Enough said I think.)

'The river at the bottom of the garden provided great
entertainment too. Foxy Lady caught a duck one day and sat on it. I
looked out of the window and wondered what on earth she was sitting
on. I went out to find it was a huge fully grown duck, much bigger

*No amount of hissing
or pecking ever
bothered Foxy.*

than she was. The duck was just sitting there unable to move
because Fox had got it by the neck. I don't think she quite knew
what to do with it next, so I rescued it from her, made sure it was all
right, and off it went, apparently unharmed.

'Whenever a swan came waddling up the garden from the river,
Smudgey, and Fox, would sniff it up the backside quite casually, and
then clout it. They were forever clouting swans, especially as they
sailed past on the water. Smudge used to clout the swans on the
back of the head as they went sedately past. No claws out . . . just a
quick clip round the ear to let them know she was there and in
charge of her bit of river bank. No amount of hissing from the swans
ever seemed to worry the cats.'

Kipper, on the other hand, was a bit more nervous
of them. She would hide behind a 'No Mooring' sign we
had, and fondly imagine the swans couldn't see her. The
funny thing is, she never seemed to know what to do next,
so she never did anything.

'Kipper went and fell in the river, and, because we had
netting hanging down, she managed to crawl out. I picked her
up and wrung her out, which sent our gardener off into absolute
hysterics!'

How could you wring a cat out?

'Well, I just held her head from behind, finger and thumb
under her jaw, one from either side, and ran the
other hand down like skinning a bunch of currant
grapes, squeezing all the water out. The
gardener had never seen anything like it in his
life. Oh he did laugh! It was lovely to see.'

Kipper's 'duck-watching' hide.

Cat Names

People ask us how we choose the names for our cats.
'If I can, I like to call them after other animals.
Beetle, Bugs, Toad, Ratty, Mouse, Mole, Foxy and
Kipper . . .'
Although a kipper is an animal that's been mucked
around with slightly more than somewhat!

'True, anyway, those are some of our cats' names over the
years. Other names just suggest themselves when you look at the
cat. Fluffy Britches, a farm kitten that was given to us, had legs
covered in orange-coloured fur. Smudge had what looked like
mascara smudged across her nose and mouth. Cloudy was a lovely
blue-grey Persian.

'I don't know how we named Wicked Weed. She was the only
surviving one of Cloudy's three kittens from some liaison that we
don't speak about. One of them was a blue, and I was heart broken
when she died. I love blue cats.'

We were away when that happened. Alwen's Dad was looking
after the house and the cats, and suddenly one of Cloudy's kittens
was dead. It would have to be the only blue one! Her father was
shattered, knowing how Alwen loved the little thing. He got the vet
in, and apparently Cloudy was totally unable to feed her kittens. They
were getting nothing from the suckling.

Unfortunately, it was already too late for the second one too, but
Alwen's father managed to save the third one, a little silky-coated
black thing. I think her experience of having this man forcibly feeding

*Baby Beetle smelling
blossoms in the
greenhouse looks for all
the world like a kangaroo.*

•

*Kipper sits amongst
the gum leaves.*

Bugs inside one of our mirror glass windows.

•

Tiger in a dark corner of the garden.

her with an eye dropper put Weed off men for life. She would always run a mile when I came anywhere near. Any man scared her.

Tiger must have had a much worse experience. He was found and brought home by Bindi and a friend of hers, and was a badly battered kitten. How *can* people ill treat them?

Even now, years later when he's a fully grown, well-fed, loved cat, you have only to touch him anywhere near his ears, and he flinches, ducks his head with his eyes clenched shut, and runs in a panic.

He tolerates me now, and is reservedly cuddly sometimes. His behaviour is fascinating when he sometimes lets me pick him up. Picture him lying on his back in my arms, this great big tabby cat. If I get my face anywhere near, to sniff him (our friendship gesture to all our cats), he puts his paw firmly on the centre of my nose and pushes me back.

I'm aware that his claws are out, but he doesn't attempt to break the skin. I know what he means. 'It's taking me all my courage to let you get as near as this to my head. I've only let you come this close because I like you and sort of trust you a bit. Don't come any closer or I may scratch you in my panic to get away, and I wouldn't want to do that.'

Poor old Tiger. He's terrified of any other man. You wonder what sort of bloke it was who could have bashed a little kitten so badly.

Fluffy poses in the garden.

•

Cloudy beautifully backlit by the sun.

Weed and Fluffy curled up in a bean cushion, and two shots of Toffee as a youngster.

*Purr Shah Pudding
sunning herself.*

Baby Ratbag secure in a box – look at those ears!

•

Foxy takes her ease on a shelf right above the heater.

Cloudy

Cloudy in the sunshine and mesmerized by a black panther on television.

Cloudy we found in Harrods pet shop. There was this gorgeous blue kitten. Alwen has always had a passion for blue cats, and so home we came with Cloudy. She didn't *do* very much as a cat. She did love to watch television, especially wildlife programmes. There was one memorable occasion when she was quite a youngster, when she was attracted by the sound of a black panther's voice coming from the television screen.

She moved sedately across (she never scampered, even as a kitten), sat herself down and watched the whole of the hour-long programme about big cats. It was fascinating watching her watching and listening to those sleek, lovely animals. I took about a dozen shots of the scene in the low-light situation, and just hoped that one or two of them would come out. Cloudy was motionless, transfixed, so she was all right in every picture, but quite a few of the shots had blurred action on the screen, as I was shooting at a very slow speed.

When Cloudy had her three kittens, Fluffy was also the proud mother of her own litter. They used to sit with their kittens all around them, and Fluffy was quite happy to take over the mothering duties. Cloudy wasn't much of a mum really. It was all too much bother for her.

We lost old Cloudy in a stupid way. I've never been able to forgive myself really, because my dad instilled into my brother

and me that we should look ahead for accidents that might happen, and take steps in advance to prevent them happening.

When she was quite a middle-aged cat we moved to our present home, right beside the river, and there was a little section that had housed a boat at one stage. Now it was solidly boarded up at water level so that there was no way into it from the river. What this effectively did was to leave a small boat-sized oblong of water, with four vertical sides, in the middle of the decking by the river's edge.

The whole family of cats that we brought with us had a very nervous time getting used to their new surroundings, but eventually they were quite at ease, and would wander anywhere at will.

You've probably guessed by now that one day we came home to find Cloudy floating in that awful oblong pool. There was not a single spot she could have found to get any purchase. The claw marks showed that. Three sides were poured concrete and the fourth, vertical hard wood boards with slippery green weed growing on it.

If only (the most useless words in the English language), if only I'd thought ahead, seen the possibility, and left some long heavy plank of wood angled into the mud in a corner somewhere.

The experience chilled us all, and our very next move was to board over that space, and to drape netting down into the water, right along the rest of the river bank, in case. It's just as well we did, because both Foxy and Kipper went in, Kipper several times. That netting certainly saved their lives.

Cloudy's death was an awful, senseless thing and it gave me a dread feeling of guilt. I still go cold when I think about it, but perhaps my mentioning it may have alerted just one of you to potential dangers around your home.

Cloudy and Fluffy.

A sad footnote. The netting was no use to Purr Shah Pudding. She slipped off the end of a boat and just went under. All that Persian fur must have waterlogged her and weighed her down. We fished around for what seemed like for ever, but never found her.

Fluffy Britches as an older lady, and Cloudy looking for the fishes.

Pussy One and Two

P ussy One had been a house-warming present from friends of ours when we moved to Sydenham. Puss was a 'house-warming' cat. He was just called Pussy, until Pussy Two was given to us by two other friends who were moving to Spain. We had to call them One and Two to differentiate.

Well, Pussy One did a marvellous thing once that you would love to have captured on movie, if only you'd known he was going to do it and had been set up and ready. But of course, you rarely are. We *do* try to look ahead from the animals point of view, and sometimes we *have* caught some magic moments, just by prethinking and guessing what may happen.

However, back to Puss One. He was sitting in front of the TV screen, casually watching whatever the programme was. Suddenly, about a million seagulls took off and flew out of shot disappearing away off the left hand side of the screen.

Talk about instinctive! Before you could scratch your left nostril or adjust your kneecaps, 'Killer Kat' was airborne, ears forward, front paws out in that encircling grabbing move, claws at the ready. He went like a shot out of a gun to where his eyes told him the

Pussy One sleeps, having moved Purr Shah out of the chair.

Drawings of geriatric Pussy One and Pussy Two.

Pussy One sleeps on the car, enjoying the warmth.

darkness and concentrating like mad, but I can't hear a thing. When I finally smarten up and have the sense to switch on the light, there's the evidence. Fluffy's fur all *over* the joint.

Fluff was not seen for two days and we feared the worst, were in fact searching everywhere for her cold and lifeless remains. Lo and behold, on the third day she returneth and henceforth she ruleth mightily in the Harris household. She was definitely top cat from that moment on.

Pussy Two was known as 'The Foreman'. Whenever workmen were in the house, for whatever reason, she would get onto some vantage point, if possible above them, say on the top of a ladder, cross her front paws, and watch their every move. She used to put some of the men off. They were quite put out, felt themselves jinxed or spooked by her.

She had an owlish face, with a very big bulging forehead, which gave the impression that her eyes were on a tremendous slant. She really looked as if she was cross and fed up, and looking daggers at you. In reality she was the mildest, quietest and most self-effacing of cats. She suffered from being second in a pecking order of two. She would walk about on eggshells so as not to upset Pussy One, who would just as soon thump her as not.

She had a curious habit. Whenever she stood still anywhere, or lay in a relaxed position, she crossed her front legs slightly. Looked as if she was taking up a ballet position.

She never put on much weight, probably worrying about when Pussy One was going to attack her next. Alwen and I were both there the one and only time the 'worm turned'. Pussy Two was sitting on a low table, right near the edge, paws crossed in 'position two', minding her own business.

Pussy One wondering whether he killed the plant.

Pussy Two with her feet in the ballet position.

83

Pussy One obviously didn't see her and was strolling along, lord of all he surveyed. His path took him under this very coffee table, and, for an instant, Pussy Two was sitting directly above her persecutor, looking down on his rear end as it sedately disappeared from view. She obviously decided there would never be a better chance, and fetched him a terrific clout right up the backside!

The look of stunned shock and outraged dignity on Pussy One's face was a delight to behold.

On one occasion a baby lion from Longleat Safari Park was brought to our house for some photo session or other that a photographer had dreamed up. We got all the shots he wanted and then the young lion played for ages in the garden. Eventually we went back into the house with this little animal on a lead. We only had two cats at the time, Pussy One and Pussy Two, and they had been shut upstairs in the bedroom long before the lion was due to arrive. Alwen went up to check on them to find that Pussy Two was totally relaxed, but Pussy One was a bit 'stir crazy'.

The photographer had gone, but the man from Longleat was still there, so we got him to take the cub into another room and close the door while we spirited Pussy One through the house and out into the garden. That wasn't what he had in mind and he was most upset to be shut out.

However, back to the lion. He was brought back into the main lounge where our daughter was watching *Sesame Street* on television. I feel children pick up their attitudes from their parents, and Bindi was totally at ease with this little animal. I say little, but the truth is that in size there wasn't much to choose between the two of them. We were treated to the magical picture of this little girl lying on her tum with her elbows spread and her chin on her hands and, right alongside her, the lion cub.

It was enchanting, especially a section where the programme was dealing with numbers and a bouncing ball was moving in huge arcs across the screen. The child was counting aloud and the little lion's head was going right up and down in time with the movement as his eyes followed the progress of the ball. I didn't have any film in my camera that day (how stupid can you be), and wasn't able to capture the scene, but it was lovely to see. The lion was mesmerized by the whole programme, and I thought what a good advert that was for *Sesame Street*. It is so well constructed to cater for the short attention span of most youngsters, and the lion was no exception.

The programme had finished, and the cub, sadly, had to be taken back to Longleat. Meanwhile, Pussy One was howling away outside, most indignant because it had started to spit down with rain. We let him in and immediately he was absolutely terrified.

Pussy Two had come downstairs after being let out, and didn't take any notice at all, but old Pussy One was crawling about on his stomach, his tail up like a Christmas tree. Alwen unintentionally coughed, and the poor cat shot three feet up in the air, dived behind the television set and would *not* move. There was this fearful frightened face peering out.

For the rest of that evening he crept and slunk about, checking round every corner, sniffing at everything. Any slight movement and he would jump a mile. It took him days to settle down. Pussy Two wasn't very bothered by this unknown smell, but what was going through the other cat's head? What did he think it was? He couldn't possibly know about lions. You'd just love to know what picture that residual scent conjured up in his mind.

A Musical Interlude

Do you remember the day Ratty and Smudge practised skating?'

No, I don't.

'You don't remember checking through all your music charts trying to organise yourself? You had music *everywhere*, on every available bit of space, all your nine-piece arrangements. I can see them now, *Sun Arise*, *Jake The Peg*, and all the rest. I think you had a long phone call in the middle of it all. Don't you remember?'

Ah . . . yes it all comes back to me. You neglected to mention that the only place I could get enough space to put all this stuff was on the floor in the hall. What a mess!

There must have been twenty or thirty different neat piles of music arranged under song titles, each with the separate charts for the piano, bass, guitar, drums – the nine different instruments. The whole floor area by the front door was covered, and I still had a great pile of music clutched in my arms.

I came off the phone to find Ratty and Smudge running the length of the hall and jumping on the music. It was like a skating rink. They would land at speed on the top bit of music, say it was the

Rats asleep and Smudgey up a gum tree.

piano chart for *Two Little Boys*. Nine pages stuck together along the edges with sticky tape and then concertina folded . . . and that would be resting on the music for all the other instruments, trumpet, trombone, alto and tenor sax, clarinet, etc. Well of course, *awayyy* they would go!

'The shiny paper was ideal. They must have thought this slippery stuff was stacked up just for their amusement.'

I recall standing open-mouthed as about three hours of organisation went down the drain in a welter of skidding paws and legs and music.

'If cats could laugh, they would have been hysterical with the fun of it all.'

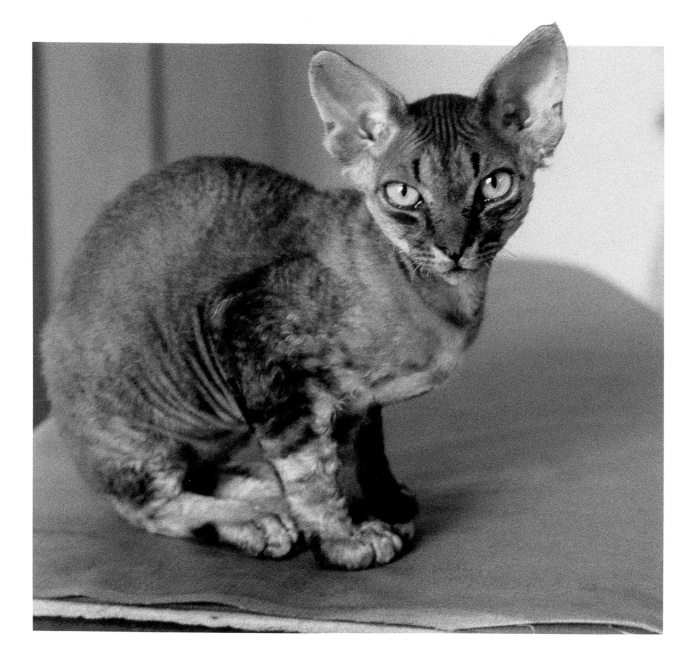

Bugsy

Bugsy gave us a heart-stopping fright almost as soon as we had him. He was exploring his new 'territory' and I had just run a bath. I'd gone into the bedroom briefly, unaware that he was anywhere near. I heard this 'plop' and idly wondering what it might be, wandered back into the bathroom. There's the poor little thing sploshing about and going up and down in the water.

If I hadn't heard that faint sound he would have been a goner! We dried him and cuddled him and he was shivering with fright all the while. You've got to have eyes in the back of your head with Rex kittens. It was so nearly a case of 'curiosity killed the cat'.

You get some enchanting things happening with these cats though. One spring a year or so back, a pair of long-tailed tits were building a nest in our garden. I must explain that our bedroom windows have a slight mirror surface on the outside, so that in the day time, you can't see in.

One day, the male bird of this pair happened to catch sight of his reflection. Of course he immediately recognised it as a really good looking rival for the affections of his lady love, and attacked. What else would a self-respecting nest builder do?

These attacks, which from then on started at first light and went on at any time during daylight hours, consisted of a rapid series of 'taps' on the glass. Sounded like a noisy toy machine gun.

Bugsy, who used to sleep in bed with us curled up in the crook of Alwen's arm, was out of bed like a shot that first day, and over to

Bugsy as a kitten. (He point blank refused to do the ironing!)

91

the window. There he stood on his hind legs on the bottom windowsill ledge, trying like mad to get the bird. Because of the mirrored effect, the bird couldn't see the cat, but the cat could see (and hear) the bird, just on the other side of the glass. You'd swear it was a Warner Brothers cartoon.

Well, we couldn't sleep of course, and this ornithological assault became a regular routine. Bugs would use some internal alarm to get himself up in the pitch dark, position himself between the curtains and the glass of the window, and wait for his unattainable prey to arrive with first light. And he did, regular as clockwork! Sometimes I would take pity on the cat and get up and move the curtains back a bit. Then, he would hop up on the chest of drawers to see round the edge of the curtain, and be at exactly the same level as that bird.

At any time through the daylight hours it would go on. There's a little weeping tree about ten feet from the window in question. This pestilential buzzard would flit in from somewhere, land on the top branch and check on the reflection of the tree in the window. Shock, horror! Over there is his hated rival peering back at him, and the fight is on again!

We would be somewhere else in the house and wouldn't hear the rapid tapping, but Bugsy would, and he would suddenly hare off in the direction of the bedroom. If you followed, you'd find him sat up on the chest of drawers, as close as he could get to the glass. There, about an inch away, on the outside, this tiny little bundle of aggression is perched on the window ledge battering away like a steam hammer with his beak. How he didn't bend it, or drive it backwards into his brain, I'll never know.

As for Bugs, well, it was better than television any day. He was thoroughly entertained in the comfort of his own home for a whole season. I shot miles of videotape of it all from every conceivable angle, from inside and out, under any and every light condition. You know, such is the crazy nature of my life that I've never managed to get the time to see that video played back. I must do it one day because it certainly was a wonderful experience – if you discount a whole springtime full of lack of sleep and ludicrously early mornings.

Post Script: The bird's obsession became such that his wife left him, he never ever got the nest built, and the last we heard of him, he'd joined some order of 'Tappist' monks. Bugs kept his appointment with destiny for month after month, but eventually the sad message got through. His little adversary was not going to be coming back.

It is quite amazing that the following spring, Bugsy took up station by the window, starting early, early in the morning, and was there waiting, every day, for weeks on end. Eventually he gave up, but it was quite moving for both of us to watch.

Sharing our lives with Devon Rexes has been the most wonderful experience, and we shall go on sharing our lives with this breed and all our other PERSONALITY CATS.

Bugs found bird watching better than television any day.